CONTENTS

INTRODUCTION

The charming castle at Hever, situated in the heart of idyllic countryside, has a rich and varied history dating back more than 700 years. Yet much of what visitors see today is the result of the remarkable efforts of a wealthy American, William Waldorf Astor, who used his fortune to restore and extend the Castle in the early 20th century, and to assemble its magnificent collection of antique portraits, furniture and tapestries.

The present peaceful setting also makes it all the more extraordinary that this quiet castle in Kent once formed the backdrop to a sequence of tumultuous events that changed the course of Britain's monarchy, religion and, indeed, history. The original medieval defensive castle with its gatehouse and walled bailey was built here in 1270 and grew in the 15th and 16th centuries to be the home of one of the most powerful families in the country, the Bullens, who added the Tudor dwelling within the walls. The Castle was to become the childhood home of Hever's most famous inhabitant, Anne Boleyn, King Henry VIII's second wife, who became Queen of England for just 1,000 days. It was Henry's love for Anne and her insistence that she became his wife rather than remain his mistress that led to the King renouncing Catholicism and creating the Church of England.

Hever Castle later passed into the ownership of another of Henry VIII's wives, Anne of Cleves, and from 1557 onwards it was owned by a number of families including the Waldegraves, the Humphreys and the Meade Waldos. It gradually fell into decline but in 1903 W.W. Astor invested vast amounts of time, money and imagination, restoring the Castle, building the adjoining 'Astor Wing' and creating the magnificent gardens and lake. At Hever, his wealth and vision enabled him to create a lavish family home that also indulged his passion for history.

The picturesque castle at Hever formed the unlikely backdrop to a sequence of tumultuous events that changed the course of Britain's history, monarchy and religion.

Top: Machicolations – one of the medieval defence methods.
Far left: Timber-framed walls from the Tudor section.
Left: The Castle's Astor Wing added 1903–8 to look like a Tudor village.

Adjacent, left to right: Silver-plated clock, c.1900, a replica of Henry VIII's wedding gift to Anne Boleyn; Tudor rose ceiling detail; 17th-century-style Spanish walnut and brass warming table, used for keeping food warm by placing embers in the lower bowl; Italian walnut carving in the elaborate balcony above the hall.

INNER HALL

The splendour of the reception room that greets visitors to Hever today forms a complete contrast to its original use in Tudor times when this was the Great Kitchen, complete with a large fireplace for cooking and a water well.

The panelling and richly carved columns are made of Italian walnut. The gallery above the hall was inspired by the screen in King's College Chapel, Cambridge, and was executed in 1905 by W.S. Frith as part of W.W. Astor's restoration of 1903–8. The chandelier suspended from the ornate ceiling is 20th-century silver, a copy of an 18th-century design from an original at Knole House in Kent.

The Inner Hall now houses a fine collection of antique furniture, which dates mostly from the 17th and 18th centuries, and many fine paintings. On the walls are portraits of three generations of Tudor monarchs: Henry VII, Henry VIII and Edward VI. The painting hanging to the left of the fireplace is of Anne Boleyn and, to the right, is her older sister, Mary. The oldest piece of furniture in the Inner Hall stands in the window bay. The walnut *cassapanca* or marriage chest dates from c.1550. It is the Tudor equivalent of a 'bottom drawer' and was used for storing garments, documents and valuables collected during an engagement, but it also doubled as a seat.

The clock on the mantelpiece is a 20th-century replica of Henry's wedding gift to Anne Boleyn. The original belonged to Horace Walpole in the 18th century. It was bought by the Keeper of the National Gallery for the Queen in the 20th century.

Above: Mary Bullen, older sister of Anne Boleyn, after Holbein. Left: Early-18th-century Aubusson tapestry from Limousin, France. Opposite: Mid-18th-century bronze statuette of Henry VIII. Overleaf: The Inner Hall.

DRAWING ROOM

Forming a light and airy contrast to the preceding room, the Drawing Room is one of the beautiful rooms created by William Waldorf Astor, who lavishly entertained his guests here, as did his descendants in later years: it was in this room that visitors would have had drinks before dinner. The Astors were renowned for their hospitality. House party guest lists, correspondence and photographs show that they socialised with royalty, prime ministers and many famous people such as Queen Elizabeth II, Winston Churchill, Sir Arthur Conan Doyle, and George Bernard Shaw, to name but a few.

When designing and creating this room and, indeed, all the rooms in the Castle, W.W. Astor paid great attention to detail and insisted that his workmen used, as far as possible, the same materials and tools as Tudor craftsmen 400 years earlier. The 20th-century craftsmen were not even allowed to use straight edges and had to do all the work by eye including the elaborate ceilings. The fine panelling in the Drawing Room was inspired by the beautiful Elizabethan panelling at Sizergh Castle, Cumbria.

W.W. Astor managed to harmonize history with 20th-century convenience and comfort and there are several interesting items in this room illustrating this success, including a semi-circular satinwood George III commode that has been converted to take a record player and a secret door in one panel that conceals a drinks cabinet. There is also a Blüthner baby grand piano in rosewood satin finish, c.1922, whilst the impressive carpet, c.1890–1900, is from Eastern Turkestan and took around eight years to make by a huge team of people.

With the exception of one duplicate, all of the beautiful panels in the elegant Drawing Room are different, and were made from oak, bog-oak and holly in 1905. One hides a secret door that leads to a turret – the Astor family hid the drinks cabinet in there!

Far left: Detail of inlaid wood panelling.
Left: View of Drawing Room with its magnificent Khotan carpet and fine furniture.

One of Henry VIII's elaborate locks on the Dining Hall doors.

DINING HALL

This splendid room was the Great Hall during the Bullens' time. It was originally open to the roof rafters but, in 1506, Thomas Bullen added a Long Gallery above it. The Bullen family would have dined here and entertained Henry VIII and his retinue when he visited. One of the impressive gilt door locks on the doors in this room belonged to Henry VIII; the other is a replica. Henry VIII was paranoid about assassination so, to ensure his safety when visiting other houses, he brought his personal locksmith to fix a special door lock to his bedchamber.

William Waldorf Astor restored and enhanced the hall by commissioning Nathanial Hitch to install the linenfold panelling and elaborately carved Minstrels' Gallery which rests fittingly on a series of carved minstrels. The impressive fireplace is of Clipsham stone from Rutland, and is surmounted by the Bullen arms.

The paintings are of the historical figures of Henry V and the Black Prince by Benjamin Burnell (fl. 1790–1828). Henry V (r. 1413–22) was victor of the Battle of Agincourt in 1415 during the Hundred Years War. Henry gained both France and the French princess, Catherine of Valois, as his wife. The Black Prince, Edward the Prince of Wales (1330–76), was a commander with victories at the Battles of Crecy and Poitiers.

The large tapestry is from a series entitled *Months and Seasons* (August) and was woven in Brussels in about 1540. Such tapestries would have taken many years to make and would have been very expensive.

The ornate carving at Hever is one of its greatest glories – from the simple to the elaborate, all the work has been executed by craftsmen who were masters of their art, whether from Tudor times or from the 20th century.

Adjacent, left to right: Bullen coat of arms carved in the fireplace; detail of Brussels tapestry depicting the months and the seasons, c.1540; 19th-century coloured glass bottles.

The buffet standing at the back of the room is oak dating from the 17th century and the coloured glass bottles and decanters are 19th century.

The Dining Hall, with its beautiful table and chairs, is still used for private and corporate functions today. The 24 walnut armchairs are Flemish, mid-17th-century style, and were sympathetically reupholstered in 2000. They surround the 17-foot (5.2 m) oak table, which dates from around 1600, although its top is a 20th-century replacement.

In the doorframe, as you leave the hall, there is a marker to the left showing the height of floodwaters that rushed into the Castle on 15 September 1968 after a tremendous storm. The waters were waist-deep in places and much of the ground floor was devastated.

Above: *The Yule Log* by Robert Alexander Hillingford (1825–1904), showing the Dining Hall before restoration and before the installation of the Minstrels' Gallery by Astor.
Left: A Green Man, carved into a beam concealed high up in the Dining Hall.
Overleaf: The Dining Hall, now frequently used for private banquets.

ENTRANCE HALL

This Entrance Hall was added to the Tudor manor house in 1506 by Thomas Bullen. Timbers dating from the late 15th century can be seen in the earlier doorway, which is directly opposite the current entrance.

The rare suit of armour dates from the 15th century. Interesting furniture housed here includes an oak bench table, c.1610, which would have been used by monks in their tiny cells, as well as the magnificent choir stall which is Italian and made from walnut c.1480: it came from a church or possibly a cathedral. There is also a *caquetoire,* or conversation chair, from the 16th century, the seat of which was made broad enough to accommodate ladies' wide dresses and therefore allowed them to chat in comfort.

The long refectory table is Italian, c.1565, and the two large vases standing on it are Japanese Imari of about 1780. The collection of dishes and plates are various dates from 1650 to 1800.

The large leather and iron jackboots towards the end of the hall are postilions' boots and date from c.1690. A postilion was a man who rode one of a pair of horses that pulled a coach. It could be very dangerous if a leg became caught between the two horses, so each postilion wore one boot on that leg to protect himself from injury.

The two large postilions' boots in the Entrance Hall were worn by two individual men, each of whom wore one protective boot on the leg which was between the two galloping horses of a four-horse coach.

Adjacent, left to right: Choir stall detail;
15th-century suit of armour.
Imari baluster jars, c.1780.

Above: Entrance Hall with choir stall.
Right: Postilions' boots.
Far right: Carving on oak chest.

Adjacent, left to right: panelling detail, one of several faces carved in the border; Tunbridge Ware sewing box, c.1850–60, top decoration illustrating Hever Castle; Derby-style figure, one of a pair depicting spring and summer, c.1880.

LIBRARY

The delightful Library, which overlooks the moat and Anne Boleyn's orchard, originally contained 2,500 books, bound for W.W. Astor in calf and Moroccan leather, and gilt-tooled with his coat of arms. Many of these books were printed on private presses in Paris and New York during the 17th, 18th and 19th centuries. The bookcases they are held in are inspired by those owned by the diarist Samuel Pepys.

This room was probably an estate office in Tudor times and W.W. Astor tried to recreate a sense of its history when he chose it as his library: the ceiling is copied from Hampton Court Palace. The carvings are in the style of Grinling Gibbons and made from a wood called sabicu, which is harder than ebony and dense enough to sink in water. The circular mahogany 'drum' table is George IV c.1820–25 and, above the fireplace, is a portrait of Johann Jakob Astor, great-grandfather of W.W. Astor, and founder of the family's

fortune in the late 18th century.

There are many examples of locally produced Tunbridge Ware in the library, including bookends, a sewing box, tea caddies and a writing slope. They all have pictures of Hever Castle as their decoration. They are made with a tessellated mosaic technique which gives the appearance of a true mosaic, but it enabled intricate designs such as birds, and even pictures and portraits, to be relatively easily produced. It involved assembling slips of wood in bundles, following patterns drawn on squared paper. These were then glued and sliced transversely, reassembled into secondary blocks, which could be cut into a series of identical veneers and applied to the item being produced. Tunbridge Ware became a popular choice of souvenir for wealthy tourists, peaking in popularity in the 19th century when even the young Princess Victoria purchased some as gifts.

Tunbridge Ware was developed and largely made locally at Tonbridge and Tunbridge Wells. It became a popular souvenir choice for wealthy tourists, peaking in popularity in the 19th century, when even the young Princess Victoria purchased some as gifts.

Left: The Library, created by W.W. Astor.
Facing page: Library desk with lamp made from a 17th-century Italian marble column.

Right: 17th-century
marquetry table and
beech-framed mirror.

MORNING ROOM

The Morning Room was a private retiring room in Tudor times. The panelling and contents in this room date mainly from the 17th century. In the stone of the fireplace surround are carved the initials H.W., representing Henry Waldegrave, another of Hever's owners. During the reign of Elizabeth I the Catholic Waldegrave family made an interesting addition to this room: it was forbidden to say Mass, so the family would have been in trouble if they were caught with a Catholic priest on the premises. A priest hole was therefore incorporated into this corner of the Castle (where the china cupboard is now) in which the priest could hide. One of the many ghostly tales surrounding Hever suggests that one such priest perished here and that his unhappy spirit still lingers.

On display are several items that may have been used or worked by ladies in the 18th and 19th centuries. These include a spinning wheel c.1800 made of cherrywood with ivory finials and boxwood and holly inlays, and a fruitwood wool winder c.1825.

There are also some fine examples of needlework, including a mahogany pole fire screen c.1725, decorated with a needlework panel in gros and petit point. Fire screens were used as protection from the direct heat of the fire and were very popular among ladies as they prevented their complexions from becoming flushed. On the wall is a mirror which features needlework called stumpwork depicting figures of Charles II and Catherine of Braganza, as well as animals and insects, enriched with seed pearls and gold thread. It has an original walnut frame and its raised and padded style was very fashionable between the 1630s and 1680s.

Three-legged chairs were popular in the 17th century as they offered more stability on the extremely uneven floors. The chairs in the Morning Room date from 1620, 1625 and 1700.

Left: Prattware tea caddy
c.1790. Far left: Triangular,
three-legged chair.

Above: The Morning Room, with its fine carving and elaborate fireplace featuring the date 1603. Far left: Detail of fireplace. Left: Rare stumpwork mirror, c.1684.

ANNE BOLEYN

The first room that visitors enter on the upper floor is a small, simple bedroom with an original 15th-century half-domed ceiling. This room is traditionally thought to have been Anne Boleyn's as a child; she may also have shared it with her sister, Mary. Anne was probably born at Hever in around 1501 but, like many children, especially girls, her birth is not recorded. She certainly spent her childhood here, however; the Castle had been the Bullen family home since her great-grandfather, Geoffrey, bought both Hever and Blickling Hall in Norfolk, having risen from humble beginnings to become Lord Mayor of London in 1459.

Geoffrey's grandson, Thomas, (b. 1477), brought Hever to the centre of the international stage when, in 1498, he married Elizabeth Howard, daughter of the Duke of Norfolk. This was an advantageous match which made his three surviving children, George, Mary and Anne, related to royalty on their mother's side.

The painting in her bedroom shows Anne wearing her famous 'B' pendant and a daring French-style hood revealing her dark hair. She was intelligent and witty, if not traditionally beautiful and the Venetian ambassador said of her: '… not one of the handsomest women in the world. She is of middling stature, with a swarthy complexion, long neck, wide mouth, bosom not much raised, and in fact has nothing but the King's great appetite, and her eyes, which are black and beautiful'. Against the wall stands a bed head with the words 'Part of Anne Boleyn's bed from Hever 1520' carved on it. It is one of the earliest Anne Boleyn 'made-up pieces' – none of it seems to date before 1600 and it was probably put together in Victorian times when there was a revival of interest in Anne Boleyn.

The ghost of Anne Boleyn is almost as famous as the lady herself was in life, holding the record for the most sightings of any spirit. Since her execution in 1536, Anne is said to have been spotted 30,000 times in 120 locations, including Hever, Blickling and the Tower of London.

Far left: Elaborate bed head. Left: Marble bust c.1800. Italian, after Francesco Lurana. Opposite: 16th-century portrait of Anne Boleyn entitled *Regina Anglie 1534* (Queen of England), by an unknown artist, but probably the nearest likeness to Anne in the Castle. She is wearing a black dress, encrusted with pearls and gold thread, and a matching headdress in the French style, together with her famous 'B' pendant.

The Book of Hours room, with its beautiful tapestries and prayer books.

In 1509, eight years after Anne's birth, Henry Tudor, then aged 18, succeeded to the throne of England as Henry VIII. He secretly married Catherine of Aragon, the 24-year-old widow of his elder brother, Arthur, between his succession to the throne and his coronation. Their marriage – a true love-match by all accounts – produced only one child out of eight pregnancies, a daughter, who became the future Queen Mary I.

Anne Bullen spent much of her time as a child at Court, pushed forward by her ambitious father, Thomas. At the age of 13, she went for the first time to France, in the train of Henry's sister, Mary Tudor, who was to marry King Louis XII. It was whilst in France that Anne Bullen became known as Boleyn. There were no set spellings in Tudor times as few people could read or write, so Anne chose to sign herself Boleyn, probably from the more sophisticated sounding French pronunciation.

The two beautifully illuminated prayer books on display here belonged to Anne: she has written in them and they bear her signature. These personal prayer books were popular in England from the 13th century until the Reformation and earned the name 'Book of Hours' from the short services to the Virgin Mary which were read at eight fixed hours during the day – the most commonly remembered today being Matins and Vespers. They also contained a calendar of church festivals, psalms, prayers, favourite saints and services for the dead. The earliest one on display was handwritten on vellum in Bruges, c.1450, and bears the poignant inscription *Le temps viendra* (The time will come), *Je Anne Boleyn*. The other is believed to be the prayer book Anne took with her to her execution at the Tower and bears the 'Remember me' inscription shown here.

'Remember me when you do pray that hope doth lead from day to day. Anne Boleyn'. Book of Hours, *c.*1528

Left: Pages from Anne Boleyn's 'Book of Hours'.

Tapestry depicting the marriage of Princess Mary Rose to Louis XII of France, Tournai, c.1525.

The large tapestry illustrates the marriage of Princess Mary Rose (sister of Henry VIII) to Louis XII of France in 1514. Anne Boleyn and her sister Mary may be amongst the ladies depicted in the tapestry as they were present. Princess Mary was 18, whilst Louis was 52 and died three months after the marriage. Princess Mary then married her sweetheart, Charles Brandon, Duke of Suffolk. Their daughter, Frances, was Lady Jane Grey's mother.

In 1522 Thomas Bullen, who had been Ambassador in France for the previous four years, returned to England, bringing Anne with him. Her sister Mary had previously been sent home in disgrace: it is rumoured she had affairs, possibly with Francis the King of France in 1515. Anne was by now a sophisticated young woman who had spent nine years at the most splendid and exciting Court in Europe and she found Hever quite dull by comparison. She was soon appointed lady-in-waiting to Queen Catherine, during which time she fell in love with the young Lord Henry Percy. This did not please Henry, who had other plans for them both, so she was banished back to Hever, lovesick and furious. It is said that she was locked in her room for a time to prevent her communicating with Percy. Her father secured her a place at Court in the Low Countries, returning in 1525 to find her family high in the King's favour. Her father had become successively Viscount Rochford, Earl of Wiltshire, Earl of Ormonde and a Knight of the Garter.

By 1525 King Henry was desperate for a male heir. Bored with his former mistress, Mary (Anne's elder sister), he suddenly fixed his attentions on 25-year-old Anne and began to make frequent visits to Hever.

The marriage plaque on display shows the coats of arms for Boleyn/Howard and Henry VIII and Anne Boleyn. The notch taken out of each coat of arms indicates both Thomas Bullen and Henry VIII were jousting champions.

The marriage plaque.

16th-century portrait of Henry VIII,
c.1535, Anglo Flemish workshop

Right: Painting of Pope Clement *c.*1527. Pope Clement is a figure of central importance in British history, as his refusal to grant Henry VIII a divorce from Catherine of Aragon led to the break with the Church of Rome and ultimately to the Reformation.
Far right: Copy of Divorce Petition sent to Pope Clement.

When Anne caught Henry's eye she was striking to look at, intelligent, sophisticated and fashionable and, at that time, Henry was 32 years old, over six feet (1.8 m) tall, handsome, extremely athletic and very well educated. Despite a relentless courtship, Anne refused to be his mistress, saying: 'Your wife I cannot be… because you have a Queen already. Your mistress I will not be', thus forcing Henry to take action in order to be able to marry her. Henry was a Catholic and had to seek the approval of the Pope to divorce Catherine. He petitioned the Pope with one of the most legible signatures on the petition being that of George Rochford, Anne's brother. Henry was furious when the Roman Catholic Church refused and stood in the way of his plans, so he then announced that his marriage to Catherine had not been legal in the first place. He declared himself head of the Church in England, married Anne in secret and had his marriage to Catherine declared null and void. Many years of religious upheaval followed his dramatic actions, with monasteries being dissolved, English Catholics rising up against the King in the north of England and prominent men refusing to take an oath of allegiance to Henry. Thus, the Reformation was set in motion – all for the love of Anne Boleyn from Hever.

When the pregnant Anne was crowned Queen in London in June 1533, there were few cheers. Her child was born that September, a girl called Elizabeth, and Anne went on to miscarry in 1534 and again in 1536. Henry began to believe that his marriage to her was cursed and, shortly after the last miscarriage, Jane Seymour, Anne's lady-in-waiting, was moved into new quarters at Henry's palace. By May 1536, Anne was a prisoner in the Tower of London, having been accused of incest with her brother, adultery with several gentlemen from Court, witchcraft and treason. She was found guilty and sentenced to death by burning, the sentence being commuted to beheading and, as a special concession, a swordsman was brought from France to ensure that Anne's head came off quickly. She was buried in the Chapel of St Peter ad Vincula in the Tower of London, and her father, his world in ruins, died two years later and was buried in St Peter's Church, Hever, his tomb's monumental brass showing him as a Knight of the Garter. Anne's mother, Elizabeth, had already died the previous year and George, her brother, was executed before his sister on 17 May 1536.

Although Anne only reigned for 1,000 days and she failed to provide Henry with a male heir, ironically it was her daughter, Elizabeth I, who became one of the longest-reigning monarchs that England has ever had. After Anne was executed, Henry promptly married Jane Seymour – the licence was actually granted on the same day as Anne's execution – but the marriage lasted only briefly as she died.

In 1540 Henry married again, this time to the daughter of a German duke, Anne of Cleves. The marriage was agreed for political reasons and on the strength of a flattering miniature portrait by Court painter Hans Holbein. The marriage was annulled after only six months and 'the Flanders Mare', as she was nicknamed, was given Hever Castle as part of the divorce settlement.

'And thus I take my leave of the world and of you all, and I heartily desire you all to pray for me.
O Lord have mercy on me, to God I commend my soul. O Lord have mercy on me, to God I commend my soul.
O Lord have mercy on me … ' Anne Boleyn's reported final words.

Right: Robert Cecil (1563–1612), English statesman and son of William Cecil, holding the rod of Lord Treasurer. Cecil was made 1st Viscount Cranbourne by James I in 1604 and Earl in 1605 in return for his services as Elizabeth I's Secretary of State in securing James' succession to the English Crown. Far right: Embroidery detail, 18th century.

STAIRCASE GALLERY

The Staircase Gallery is the smaller of the two galleries in the Castle and was created in 1506 by Thomas Bullen over the Entrance Hall to give access between the two wings of the house and his newly built Long Gallery upstairs.

There is an impressive portrait of Anne Boleyn's daughter Elizabeth I (r. 1558–1603). Elizabeth was the last Tudor monarch and, as she never married, succession then passed to James I (VI) of Scotland, son of Mary Queen of Scots.

The delightful baby clothes in the cabinet are complemented by a panelled oak cradle with a domed canopy and child's high chair that date to around 1625. There is also a collection of items purchased from Ashridge House, Hertfordshire, including 17th-century silk embroidered personal possessions, such as indoor slippers, brushes, a night cap, purse and comb case.

The silk baby clothes on display were originally thought to date from Tudor times and were bought by the Astor family in 1923 from a sale at Ashridge House, Berkhamsted, Herts. In 1998, an infestation of carpet beetle in the showcase prompted conservation treatment and, on closer inspection, they were found to be late 17th century to early 18th century.

Far left: Overview of room. Left: 17th-century embroidered gentlemen's shoes. Facing page: Elizabeth I, (r. 1558–1603), c.1580.

KING HENRY VIII'S BEDCHAMBER

This room is named after King Henry VIII's visits to the Castle, although it is impossible to know for certain in which room he slept. However, it is one of the largest bedchambers in the Castle and so was restored by the Astor family to be fit for a King of Henry's importance and proportions. It is true to say that the Castle's best rooms would have been prepared for the King and hosting him and his retinue would have been a large burden for any household, but particularly for a relatively small one like Hever.

The magnificent bed in this room with its blue velvet hangings is certainly the type that the monarch would be used to: it dates from 1540 and is a 'tester' bed, tester being the name for the solid wooden canopy suspended above it. By the fire hangs a Dutch brass warming-pan dating from the 18th century, which would have been used as an early form of bed heating in an otherwise cold and draughty Castle. The pan would have been filled with hot embers and passed under the bedclothes to heat and air the bed. The earliest known example of this method of heating beds was made in 1616.

The ceiling in the bedchamber is the oldest in the Castle dating from around 1462 and the panelling from 1565, with the exception of the section over the fireplace which commemorates the two wives of Henry VIII who lived at Hever Castle – Anne Boleyn and Anne of Cleves.

Far left: Detail of carved bedpost.
Left: 18th-century French Regency-style wardrobe and window.

Above: Impressive tester bed made of finely carved oak c.1540. Left: Panel detail over the fireplace which commemorates Henry VIII, Anne Boleyn and Anne of Cleves.

Right: Detail of French walnut
chest front, c.1505, depicting
scenes from Genesis.

WALDEGRAVE ROOM

This room is named after the Waldegrave family who lived at Hever through the reign of the last of the Tudor monarchs and into the Stuart dynasty. When the Catholic Queen Mary I (eldest daughter of Henry VIII) came to the throne in 1553, the Waldegraves were in Royal favour. In 1557, after the death of Anne of Cleves, Sir Edward Waldegrave was appointed one of the Commissioners to sell any land which the Crown had seized and promptly assigned the Castle to himself. It was to remain in the possession of the Waldegrave family for over 158 years, longer than any other owner of the Castle. When Queen Mary died and Elizabeth came to the throne in 1558, Edward and his son Charles were deprived of all their appointments. Charles, very prudently, retired to Hever and in 1584 the small chapel, or oratory, was built, hidden behind panelling so he could practice his faith in secret.

In 1683, Henry Waldegrave married Henrietta FitzJames, the illegitimate daughter of James, Duke of York, pictured in this room. With the accession to the throne of King James II,

the first Catholic monarch since the days of Queen Mary, Henry's fortune seemed assured and he was created the 1st Baron Waldegrave. A future of high office seemed likely, but the new wind, for which the Waldegraves had waited so long, proved fickle: the country would not accept a Catholic King, Prince William of Orange landed at Torbay and King James fled to France. Henry collected a large sum of money which he took to the King in Paris, but he died there the following year.

Henry's son, James (named after the King), had however, learned a long and painful lesson. Catholics were out of favour and likely to remain so, so he renounced his faith, took the Oath of Supremacy, conformed to the Church of England and took his seat in the House of Lords. It proved to be an advantageous move. He was appointed Ambassador to France in 1725 and, in 1729, was elevated to the Earldom of Waldegrave. In 1735 he became a Privy Councillor. The little castle at Hever proved too small to match his growing status, so, in 1715, he sold it to Sir William Humphreys, a former Lord Mayor of London.

The Rhyming Blade Sword in the cabinet is one of only five known to exist and was created in support of the 1745 Jacobite Rebellion. Figures of James III and various saints are engraved on each side of the blade and it bears the inscription: 'With this sword thy cause I will maintain; And for thy sack (sake) O James breath (break) each vein.'

Far left: The Waldegrave Room with its French oak and walnut four-poster bed, c.1485. Left: The Oratory Chapel with its 19th-century painting of the Virgin in ecstasy above the Spanish altar. Facing page: Italian rock crystal Cross mounted in gilded bronze.

Portraits of Henry VII c.1506 and Elizabeth of York, late
16th century. Henry VII and Elizabeth were the parents of
Henry VIII: their marriage united the houses of Lancaster and
York after Henry VII took the throne by force by defeating
Richard III at the Battle of Bosworth in 1485, ending many
years of conflict known as the Wars of the Roses.

LONG GALLERY

The Long Gallery is more than 98 feet (30 m) long and runs the entire width of the building. The Long Gallery is an architectural term given to a long, narrow room, often with a high ceiling. They were usually located on the upper floor of the great houses at the time. This one was created in 1506 by Thomas Bullen who put a ceiling over the Great Hall below. They served several purposes: among others, they were used for entertaining guests, for taking exercise in the form of walking when the weather was inclement, and for displaying art collections. Tradition has it that Henry VIII held Court in the alcove at the far end of the Long Gallery when he visited the Castle.

The panelling in the gallery is Elizabethan and the ceiling is a 16th-century-style reproduction executed for W.W. Astor.

The four beautiful chandeliers are copies of originals at Hampton Court Palace and the stained glass in the windows shows the coats of arms of successive owners of the Castle. The views from the Long Gallery include, from the east end, the Tudor gardens and topiary cut to the shape of a medieval-style chess set. The west windows look over Anne Boleyn's Orchard, which is a riot of yellow daffodils in the spring.

Today, the Long Gallery, and indeed the whole Castle, is home to a collection of some of the most important Tudor paintings anywhere in the country, including portraits of all of Henry VIII's wives, children and closest relatives.

Portraits were extremely important in Tudor times as few people could read or write and may never have had the chance

The coats of arms in the stained glass commemorate the different owners of Hever Castle since it was built. They include at the west end the coat of arms of Sir John Fastolf who owned the Castle 1408–23. Fastolf was later characterised as Falstaff by William Shakespeare in *Henry IV*, *Henry V* and *The Merry Wives of Windsor*.

Above: *The Falconry Party*, 1861, by Robert Alexander Hillingford (1825–1904), showing the old stone bridge at Hever.
Left: Painting of the Long Gallery, 1861.

View of the Long Gallery.

to see the country's monarch in person. The portraits reveal a lot about the sitters and how they wished to be perceived, and are not necessarily true likenesses of the people they portray. It is probably fair to say that many of the paintings were, in fact, 'airbrushed' or enhanced, to illustrate the attractiveness, wealth and status of the sitters, using jewels, rich clothing and other props.

The portrait of Henry VIII's older brother Arthur, c.1500, was unveiled by eminent historian Dr David Starkey in 2006, as 'the only surviving portrait of Arthur that could have been painted in his lifetime,' meaning that it is one of the earliest surviving easel portraits in British art. As with many Tudor paintings, the picture is rich in symbolism: the white gillyflower Arthur is holding is probably a symbol of his betrothal to Catherine of Aragon (she was Arthur's wife before becoming Henry's), as well as his purity (by reason of its colour) and his kingship (represented by the coronet-like shape of its flowers).

Also in the Castle is a painting of Cardinal Wolsey c.1675, the only known portrait type of the cardinal that has a claim to derive from a portrait executed in his lifetime.

Wolsey is shown in his cardinal's robes, holding a document which may well represent the Papal Bull appointing him as cardinal. The charges on his coat of arms allude to his personality, the rose refers to his Tudor patronage, the lion to Pope Leo X who made him cardinal and the choughs (birds) to the arms of St Thomas a Becket. The blue leopard's head may be borrowed from the de la Pole Earls of Suffolk, in which county Wolsey was born.

Careful restoration of some of Hever's paintings has also revealed that some were altered and over-painted at different times. Indeed, the portrait of Henry VIII, c.1535 (pictured page 26), which was unveiled in 2004, revealed a younger face after restoration, shown in a three-quarter profile beneath the mask of the older tyrant. It is possible that the image of the older Henry painted by Holbein became the standard picture of the monarch and hence the painting was 'updated'. The softer version of Henry that has been uncovered may have been more like the Henry that Anne Boleyn knew, as they were married around the date it was painted. Another portrait that has been shown to have been altered in the 19th century is that of Catherine of Aragon. It was restored in 1999 and found to have been previously repaired and enlarged; only the central panel was original to the 16th century. Later additions, including a gold necklace and differently shaped headdress, were removed during the restoration, leaving only the original painting.

In the unusual portrait of Elizabeth I painted when she was 25, in 1558, the year she came to the throne, she is painted in the likeness of her father, an inference perhaps that she too would be a good monarch. The larger image of Elizabeth I (pictured page 29) housed in the Castle became the more well known image of her. It is contrived to show her as a glorious leader but, like her father Henry VIII and her grandfather Henry VII, she thoroughly understood both the necessity and the methods of effective propaganda.

'Hever Castle, once the home of that great figure of Tudor history, Anne Boleyn, now has one of the best collections of Tudor portraits after the National Portrait Gallery.' David Starkey

THE TUDORS

Lady MARGARET BEAUFORT = (1) EDMUND TUDOR
(sole heiress) d. 1509   Earl of Richmond, son of Owen Tudor
by Catherine, widow of King Henry V
(2) Sir HENRY STAFFORD
(3) THOMAS STANLEY
Lord Stanley became 1st Earl
of Derby

Catherine of Aragon   Anne Boleyn

HENRY VII = ELIZABETH OF YORK
1485–1509 | (d. 1503) daughter of Edward IV

ARTHUR = CATHERINE
Prince of   of Aragon
Wales KG
(d. 1502)

Above: Rare portrait of Prince Arthur, c.1500. Arthur was the older brother of Henry VIII. Arthur's early death changed the course of history: as the eldest it was he who had been heir to the throne.

Right: Portrait of Henry VIII, c.1535, Anglo-Flemish workshop. Henry VIII (r. 1509–47) is probably England's best-known monarch, famous for his bloodthirsty actions and having six wives. Many of his actions were an attempt to secure a Tudor male heir to the throne. His desperation came as his own claim to the throne was tenuous, it having been taken by force by his father and, historically, no female monarch had ever successfully reigned in her own right.

HENRY VIII = (1) CATHERINE of = (2) ANNE
1509–47   Aragon, (d. 1536)   daughter of
daughter of   Thomas Boleyn,
Ferdinand V, first   Earl of Wiltshire,
King of Spain and   executed 1536
widow of Arthur,
Prince of Wales
(divorced 1533)

MARY I = PHILIP II
1553–58   King of Spain, son of
Emperor Charles V

ELIZABETH I
1558–1603

Portrait of Elizabeth I, 1558, English School

1 Portrait of **Catherine of Aragon**, 16th-century English School. Divorced. Catherine of Aragon (1485–1536), Henry's first and longest reigning Queen had previously been married at the age of 16 to Henry's older brother, Arthur. After many pregnancies, the only surviving child from her marriage to Henry was a girl, Mary. Catherine, a devout Catholic, refused to accept her subsequent divorce from Henry and so was forced to live in humble conditions and apart from her daughter until she died. Her acceptance never came and, before she died at the age of 50, she signed her last letter 'Catherine the Queen'.

2 Portrait of **Anne Boleyn**, c.1550, holding a red rose. Beheaded. Anne Boleyn (1501–36), Queen for 1,000 days, whose story is told in this guidebook.

3 Portrait of **Jane Seymour**, 16th century after Holbein. Died. Jane Seymour (1507/8?–37) was lady-in-waiting to Anne Boleyn; she became engaged to Henry the day after Anne's execution and married him ten days later. She gave birth to a son, the future King Edward VI, but died of complications shortly afterwards. When Henry died, he asked to be buried alongside Jane.

4 Portrait of **Anne of Cleves**, 16th century, after Barthel Bruyn the Elder. Divorced. Anne of Cleves (1515–57), the daughter of a German duke, who Henry married for political reasons and on the basis of a miniature portrait by the Court painter, Holbein. When the pair met, however, Henry was shocked at how Anne really looked and by her lack of education. It was too late to cancel the marriage but Henry had it annulled after six months. Anne was given Hever Castle as part of the divorce settlement and eventually enjoyed a happy, platonic relationship with the King who called her 'sister'.

5 Portrait of **Catherine Howard**, 16th century, follower of Holbein. Beheaded. Catherine Howard (1521?–42) was Anne Boleyn's cousin and came to Court as a lady-in-waiting to Anne of Cleves. She was sentenced to death for treason and was beheaded at the Tower of London. Her reported final words were 'I die a Queen, but I would rather have died the wife of Culpepper,' Culpepper being the name of one of her lovers.

6 Portrait of **Catherine Parr**, c.1528, English School. Survived. Catherine Parr (1512–48), had been married and widowed twice before and had just begun a romance with Thomas Seymour, Jane Seymour's brother, when Henry took a liking to her. When Henry died only four years later, Catherine married her old love, Thomas Seymour. By then she was in her mid-thirties and had had no children, despite four marriages. She finally fell pregnant, but died the following year from complications.

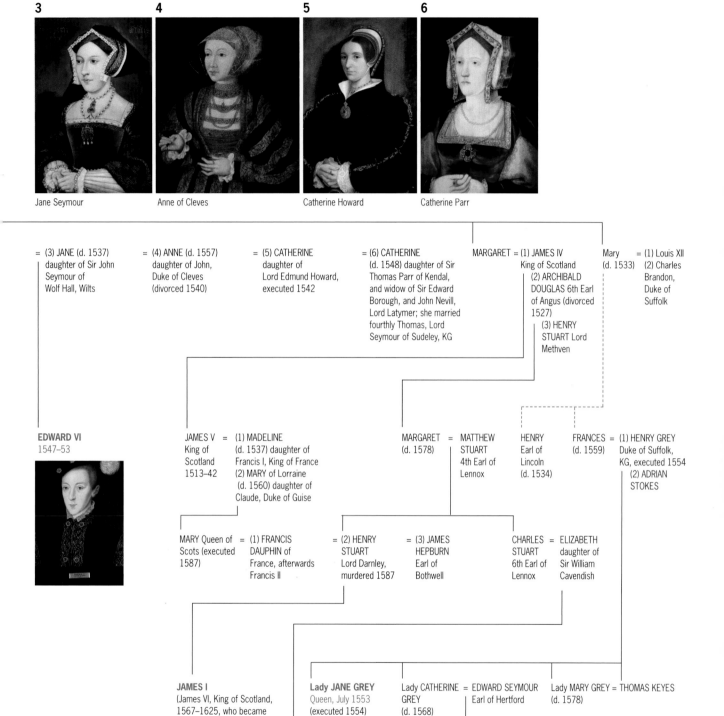

3 Jane Seymour

4 Anne of Cleves

5 Catherine Howard

6 Catherine Parr

= (3) JANE (d. 1537)
daughter of Sir John
Seymour of
Wolf Hall, Wilts

= (4) ANNE (d. 1557)
daughter of John,
Duke of Cleves
(divorced 1540)

= (5) CATHERINE
daughter of
Lord Edmund Howard,
executed 1542

= (6) CATHERINE
(d. 1548) daughter of Sir
Thomas Parr of Kendal,
and widow of Sir Edward
Borough, and John Nevill,
Lord Latymer; she married
fourthly Thomas, Lord
Seymour of Sudeley, KG

MARGARET = (1) JAMES IV
King of Scotland
(2) ARCHIBALD
DOUGLAS 6th Earl
of Angus (divorced
1527)
(3) HENRY
STUART Lord
Methven

Mary   = (1) Louis XII
(d. 1533)   (2) Charles
Brandon,
Duke of
Suffolk

EDWARD VI
1547–53

JAMES V = (1) MADELINE
King of   (d. 1537) daughter of
Scotland   Francis I, King of France
1513–42   (2) MARY of Lorraine
(d. 1560) daughter of
Claude, Duke of Guise

MARGARET = MATTHEW
(d. 1578)   STUART
4th Earl of
Lennox

HENRY   FRANCES = (1) HENRY GREY
Earl of   (d. 1559)   Duke of Suffolk,
Lincoln   KG, executed 1554
(d. 1534)   (2) ADRIAN
STOKES

MARY Queen of = (1) FRANCIS
Scots (executed   DAUPHIN of
1587)   France, afterwards
Francis II

= (2) HENRY
STUART
Lord Darnley,
murdered 1587

= (3) JAMES
HEPBURN
Earl of
Bothwell

CHARLES = ELIZABETH
STUART   daughter of
6th Earl of Sir William
Lennox   Cavendish

JAMES I
(James VI, King of Scotland,
1567–1625, who became
first Sovereign in England of
the House of Stuart, 1603)

Lady JANE GREY
Queen, July 1553
(executed 1554)

Lady CATHERINE = EDWARD SEYMOUR
GREY   Earl of Hertford
(d. 1568)

Lady MARY GREY = THOMAS KEYES
(d. 1578)

EDWARD SEYMOUR = HONORA
Lord Beauchamp   daughter of
(d. 1612)   Sir Richard
Rogers

THOMAS SEYMOUR = ISABEL
(d. 1600)   ONLEY

(1) Lady ARABELLA = WILLIAM SEYMOUR = (2) FRANCES
STUART   Duke of   daughter of Robert
(d. 1615)   Somerset, KG   Devereux, Earl of Essex
(d. 1660)

from whom descends HM Queen
Elizabeth The Queen Mother (deceased)

Right: Green Man carved in the Astor Suite panelling. Far right: Painting of Johann Jakob Astor, 20th century, by Timothy Easton, after Gilbert Stuart (American, 1755–1828). Copy of an original oil painting dated 1794 which is in The Brook Club, New York. Johann Jakob (1763–1848) was the founder of the Astor fortune. Opposite: Walnut bureau, c.1695, with family photos.

ASTOR SUITE

This section of the Castle is dedicated to its more recent history: it contains pictures and memorabilia relating to the Astor family who were the owners for 80 years from 1903. This remarkable American family was responsible for most of what visitors see today: they restored, added to and enhanced the existing rooms and then combed the world for paintings, furniture, carpets, tapestries and objet d'art worthy to furnish and decorate their fine home.

The Astor family story is a 'rags to riches' one, just like that of the Bullens in Tudor times. In 1783, a butcher's boy called Johann Jakob Astor emigrated from the small German town of Walldorf to America. He took up fur-trading in the north-east, buying his furs from the Indian

trappers, and became more and more successful until, by the end of the 18th century, he owned a fleet of 12 merchant vessels which carried his furs to Europe and the Far East and returned with manufactured goods and tea, which he sold in America. His main base for trading was in the state of Oregon, later to be renamed Astoria in his honour. J.J. Astor was a shrewd investor in New York real estate and, when he died in 1848, he was the richest man in America. Succeeding generations extended the family interests in politics, hotels, magazines, newspapers, racehorses and agriculture.

J.J. Astor's great-grandson, William Waldorf, inherited the benefits of the original fortune and the continuing success in

Hever Castle was restored by W.W. Astor with all the comforts of Edwardian life in mind. It has bathrooms with modern plumbing, electricity and central heating but, as you walk round, you will find it hard to spot light switches, radiators or pipes, as many are carefully concealed.

Far left: Painting of William Waldorf Astor, 1892, by Leon Bonnart (French, 1832–1922), oil on canvas. William Waldorf Astor was responsible for the restoration of Hever Castle 1903–8. Left: Painting of John Jacob Astor V, 1937, by Sir Oswald Birley (British, 1880–1952). John Jacob Astor was the younger son of W.W. Astor who succeeded the ownership of Hever. He was 1st Baron Astor of Hever and is pictured here wearing *The Times* cricket blazer with the *I Zingari* cravat.

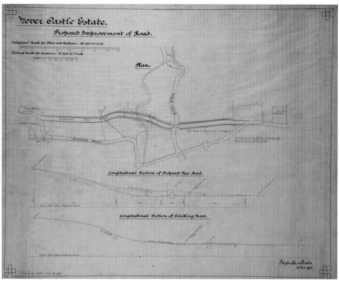

Above: Some of the 800 workers who dug the lake. Right: Plan of road improvement, part of W.W. Astor's changes in 1903–8

business and investment of the next two generations. He also developed a love for Europe, particularly when he was appointed American Ambassador to Italy between 1882 and 1885. He grew increasingly disenchanted with his native land, however, and announced publicly that 'America was no longer a fit place for a gentleman to live'. He left America for England in 1890 with a reputed 100 million dollars (the equivalent of at least ten times that amount today) and totally absorbed himself in his adopted country, buying Cliveden in Buckinghamshire in 1893 and, ten years later, Hever Castle and 640 acres of land from the Meade Waldo family.

At Hever, W.W. Astor was able to translate his historical sense and romantic taste into his own 'grand design'. He was a man of enormous energy and vision: he wanted to live in 20th-century style and comfort and to entertain lavishly but, at the same time, preserve the Castle itself and to perpetuate its historical associations.

Between 1903 and 1908, with his architect, F.L. Pearson, W.W. Astor set about building a complete 100-room wing, in the style of a Tudor village, on the far side of the Castle moat, joining the two parts with a covered bridge. The village-style wing was designed so that it could be kept to a scale that allowed the Castle to remain the dominant building, so the apparently separate cottages were constructed of varying materials, shapes, angles and styles within the whole

Detail from the Arch of Claudius. This relief was part of a much larger composition, a ceremonial procession that depicted a triumph. It was attributed to the Arch of Claudius which is dated by inscription to the year AD 51. The Emperor Claudius erected this arch in commemoration of the conquest of Britain and it was probably destroyed in the eighth century AD. The relief was purchased, along with many other articles, to furnish the Italian gardens at Hever at the turn of the 20th century by William Waldorf Astor who, at the time, was the American Minister in Rome. The relief has been re-displayed indoors in view of its age and importance.

Above: Lady Irene Astor – a Red Cross nurse, during World War II, with Churchill.
Left: View over the Castle's extensive roofline.

Tudor concept but, inside the structure, all the rooms were joined by corridors and service areas to provide sumptuous rooms for family and guests.

Cellars were built underneath the Astor Wing and part of the Castle and enormous boilers to provide hot water and central heating were installed in them. Miles of cables and pipes running through these cellars provide power, light, heat and water to the entire complex. Astor also had a fire-fighting system, a power station and a private water supply but, perhaps most amazing of all, there is an elaborate air-pressurised sewage disposal system still used today.

W.W. Astor's massive project employed an incredible 800 craftsmen, including the most skilled plasterers, carpenters, stonemasons and metal workers of their generation, and Astor visited many Tudor buildings for inspiration. In order to achieve the final design, the bed of the River Eden and the nearby public road had to be moved to create sufficient room for the village. The lake and gardens were also created; the work was largely carried out by hand with a further force of 748 workmen.

In 1916 W.W. Astor was created Baron and, in 1917, Viscount Astor. He died in 1919 and was succeeded by his elder son, Waldorf, who had been born in 1879 and educated in England. In 1905, Waldorf married the celebrated and formidable Nancy Langhorne from Virginia who famously disliked Winston Churchill, and who,

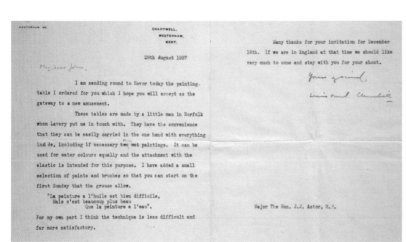

Above: Easel set, a present to J.J. Astor from Winston Churchill, who lived at nearby Chartwell. Both men were keen artists and a letter on the wall mentions the gift.

Photo of floods at Hever in 1968.

as Lady Nancy Astor, was the first woman to take her seat in the House of Commons.

W.W. Astor's younger son, John Jacob V, succeeded to ownership of Hever in 1918 after distinguished service in the Life Guards during World War I. He was MP for Dover from 1922 to 1945 and continued his father's charitable and business interests. He was elevated to the peerage in 1956 as 1st Baron Astor of Hever, and the two titles remain in the family today. He was, in turn, succeeded by Gavin, 2nd Baron of Hever, who also served in the Life Guards in World War II and later devoted his energies to the newspaper world as Chairman of the Board of The Times Publishing Company and, later, Life President of Times Newspapers Ltd. He also

carried out further improvements to the Astor Wing and in 1963 he opened the Castle and gardens to the public for the first time. Gavin was succeeded by his eldest son, John Jacob VIII, 3rd Baron Astor, in 1984.

Throughout the Astor family's association with Hever, it remained a comfortable family home, albeit a lavish one, where they could live and entertain their many guests. The homeliness is nowhere better seen than in the three small bedrooms in the Astor Suite corridor which were created in 1968 for the three daughters of the house. Each was allowed to choose their own décor and the rooms were affectionately known as the 'Dog Kennels' by the Astors.

These bedrooms were created following a disastrous event

Nancy Astor famously said to Churchill, 'Winston, if you were my husband, I'd poison your tea'. Churchill replied, 'Nancy, if I were your husband, I'd drink it'.

Gavin Astor, (2nd Baron of Hever) and Lady Irene Astor with HM Queen Elizabeth I (far left) and Margaret Thatcher (left).

in the Castle's more recent history, one that nearly obliterated much of the Astors' restoration work on the ground floor and the collections that had been lovingly gathered by them in the preceding decades. The Castle had been flooded in 1958, but a severe storm on 15 September 1968 caused more than 5 inches (12.5 cm) of rain to fall in 16 hours. Hever is situated close to the River Eden (a tributary of the Medway) and only 117.5 feet (36 m) above sea level. Consequently, water poured through about 100 rooms of the Castle and the neighbouring Astor Wing and six cottages and stables, to a depth of 4.5 feet (1.4 m). The flooding began at about 10.30 am and by 6 pm members of staff and other occupants began to be taken out of the buildings by boat and lifeline. By 9 pm the rescue was complete but the Castle's contents on the ground floor were completely ruined; some had to be destroyed on health grounds and some were sent to be restored. The walls and floors were not dried out enough to permit redecoration and refurnishing until 1970 and renovation work was not completed until 1972.

It seems that neither nature, nor history, have managed to destroy the attractive Castle visitors enjoy today.

Since 1983, the whole property has been in the ownership of the Yorkshire-based private company, Broadland Properties Limited.

Left: John Jacob Astor (1st Baron Astor of Hever) with former Prime Minister, Neville Chamberlain, opening *The Times* new printing office in 1937.
Above: John Jacob Astor VIII (3rd Baron Astor of Hever) with Nancy Reagan, wife of former US President.

GATEHOUSE

The tour of the Castle concludes in the oldest part – the medieval Council Chamber in the Gatehouse. The first 13th-century owners of the Castle would have eaten, slept and entertained here, and it also contains the *garderobe*, a 13th-century toilet which emptied directly into the moat. A raised dais with two throne-like chairs illustrates how the Lord of the Manor would have used the room for meetings and dispensing justice when it was still used as a Council Chamber.

The Gatehouse would originally have had several defence mechanisms such as a portcullis, moat, drawbridge, murder holes and machicolations, some of which are still visible. It now contains collections of historic swords and armour, as well as instruments of execution, torture and discipline,

including several German beheading swords dating from the 16th and 17th centuries. An early-18th-century torture collar with deep spikes is particularly gruesome. There is also a cast-iron man-trap from around 1800 which was used to catch trespassers and poachers; these became illegal in 1861.

The exit stairs are a defensive spiral staircase and will take you back into the Castle Courtyard where the difference in age between the 13th-century Gatehouse and timber-framed Tudor additions is most obvious. The front portcullis is said to be one of the oldest working portcullises in the country. The drawbridge was reinstated by W.W. Astor and can still be raised.

The scolds' bridles – also called branks – were designed for outspoken women who defied authority and were public nuisances. They prevented them from speaking; some had a tongue plate formed from a flat piece of iron that passively discouraged tongue movement, whilst others could be as painful as a spiked iron bit.

Far left: Scolds' bridles.
Left: Portcullis counterweights.
Facing page: View from courtyard of Gatehouse arch.

THE GARDENS

The beautiful gardens at Hever Castle were laid out between 1904 and 1908 by Joseph Cheal & Son, turning marshland into the spectacular gardens you see today and which are a pleasure to visit at any time of the year.

One of the most magnificent areas of the gardens is the Italian Garden, which was designed to display William Waldorf Astor's collection of Italian sculpture. Over 1,000 men worked on the great design with around 800 men taking two years to dig out the 38-acre (14.2 ha) lake at the far end of the Italian Garden. Within four years the 125 acres (50 ha) of classical and natural landscapes were constructed and planted. The garden is only now reaching its full maturity and includes the colourful walled Rose Garden which contains over 4,000 plants.

There are many water features around the gardens, including Half Moon Pond, the Cascade, the cool and shady grottoes, the formal Loggia fountain inspired by the Trevi fountain in Rome, and the more informal Two Sisters' Pond.

Other areas that you can stroll through include the Tudor Garden, Rhododendron Walk and Anne Boleyn's Walk, with its collection of trees planted more than 100 years ago.

In recent years, the present owners have made several changes to the gardens, including the installation of the Millennium Fountain that can be found on Sixteen Acre Island forming an interesting feature at the far end of this more informal area of the gardens. The 110-metre herbaceous border has been reinstated and Sunday Walk created, providing a peaceful woodland garden following the course of a stream. In addition to the existing Yew Maze, a splashing water maze has been built on Sixteen Acre Island – a unique feature which is especially popular with children.

With 20,000 spring bulbs planted in the gardens each year, visitors are guaranteed a breath-taking display.

Far left: White marble benitier.
Left: Castle and Astor Wing from the outer moat. Facing page: West face of the Castle from Topiary Walk.

Left: Spring border from Half Moon Pond.
Above: The Castle from the moat.
Inset below: Golden Stairs.

SPRING

Spring is a wonderful time to view the gardens at Hever: a carpet of thousands of yellow and cream daffodils welcomes visitors in Anne Boleyn's Orchard and in many other areas. There are also spectacular swathes of spring bulbs to see, such as dainty snowdrops (*Galanthus*), purple crocuses, elegant scilla, vigorous little grape hyacinths (*Muscari*), low-growing *Chionodoxa* and vivid bluebells (*Hyacinthoides non-scripta*).

The spring borders are a delight to the eye, with an impressive palette of colours created by the rhododendrons, azaleas, acers and mock orange (*Philadelphus*). In the Italian

Garden primulas, violas, wallflowers and tulips of every shape and hue create a dazzling display. This is also the time of year that the first flowering clematis, *Clematis armandii*, begins to produce its exquisite, vanilla-coloured flowers, which smell almost honey-like, against the backdrop of long, evergreen leaves.

But the gardens at Hever offer more than just a visual display – other senses are

Don't miss the wonderful Yew Maze, which has more than 1,000 individual yew trees lining its winding paths.

Far left: Large earthenware jar, about 2,000 years old, probably used for storing olive oil or water. Left: The Yew Maze. Facing page: Looking to the Castle from Rhododendron Walk.

stimulated as wonderful scents waft in the air and spring breezes rustle freshly formed foliage and the drooping heads of lilac wisteria blooms. As spring progresses, the sweet scent of the golden flowers of the azalea *Rhododendron luteum* fills the air. In the Blue Corner fragrant, deep blue,full heads of the 'King of the Blues'

hyacinth emerge under the canopy of the graceful *Ceanothus*, or Californian lilac.

In late spring the walls of the Pergola Walk are bedecked with an array of different varieties of camellia, including *Camellia sinensis*, commonly known as the tea plant whose leaves create the nation's favourite drink.

More than 15,000 bedding plants are planted in the gardens annually, ensuring a wonderful display, no matter what weather conditions the seasons bring.

Facing page: The Rose Garden. Above: Golden yew 'chess set' in Tudor Garden. Far left: Ganymede with the eagle in the Italian Garden. Left: Tulips with fluted column on Pompeiian Wall.

Far left: Rose Garden.
Left: Detail of Nymphs' Fountain, Italian Garden.
Above: Pergola, Italian Garden.
Facing page: Fountain in Tudor Garden.

SUMMER

Nothing is more quintessentially English than a rose garden in full bloom, and the roses at Hever are particularly admired, with more than 4,000 beautifully displayed bushes creating a kaleidoscope of colour and wonderfully perfumed aromas. There is an endless variety of roses in the gardens, but especially look out for the purplish, highly perfumed rose, 'Rhapsody in Blue', and the large blowsy 'Buxom Beauty', as well as the numerous *Rosa floribunda* varieties and the dramatic climbing roses. The Tudor Garden features billowing pale pink *Rosa* 'Ballerina', whilst at Half Moon Pond you can enjoy the dark red, velvety petals of *Rosa* 'Deep Secret'.

The Rose Bank on Two Sisters' Lawn is also a delight with the musky fragrances of Gallica, Bourbon, Moss and Damask roses.

As the days lengthen, the Mediterranean-style planting within the Pompeiian Wall bursts into life with exotic treats such as olives, kiwis, figs and pomegranates, all brimming with fruit. Look up and you will see the horse chestnut trees with their elevated pink and white blossom heads forming an elegant backdrop to the variety of colours and shapes that greet you at eye-level.

THE HEVER ROSE
A special Hever Castle rose is currently being developed and should be available to enjoy from 2009.

This rose will produce large heads of deep red, fading to cerise and has wonderful golden yellow stamens. In trials it has proved very resistant to disease. Surprisingly enough the Hever Castle rose has been bred using one red and one yellow rose!

Facing page: South-west gate
of Italian Garden.
Right: 15th-century carving.
Far right: Long Border.
Below: Sunday Walk.
Below right: Italian Garden.

The long border at Hever has been designed in a Gertrude
Jekyll style and displays hundreds of different perennials, each
vying for attention. Notice how the colours move from silver
and white to blue, purple, pink and then to yellow, orange and
red at the centre, before falling back through these colours to
silver and white again.

As summer progresses and then begins to fade, more than
400 dahlias begin to create their own dazzling displays of
colour at Two Sisters' Lawn, presenting an uplifting vista right
through until the first frosts of autumn appear.

The Herb Garden, which forms part of the Tudor Garden,
also looks its best in summer.

**The gardens at Hever have won an award and both the gardens and Castle have been used as television
and film sets.**

Far left: Sunken Garden.
Left: Detail of Roman
well head.

Far left: Queen Anne's Walk.
Left: Millennium Fountain.
Below: Italian Garden.

AUTUMN

Autumn is the season in which Hever's striking trees come to the fore, with the yellow, red and orange leaves of beech, liquid amber (*Liquidamber styraciflua*) and Japanese maples all contributing to an explosion of colour. Other trees and shrubs seem to compete by revealing beautifully coloured bark and stems that exhibit equally stunning autumnal colours.

The spectacular Boston ivy (*Parthenocissus tricuspidata*) that scrambles up the Castle seems to clothe the walls in a warm, colourful coat as its leaves change from green to red, whilst the dazzling purple berries of the Beauty Berry (*Callicarpa*), and the clear blue flowers which emerge amongst the striking pink, cream and green variegated leaves of the *Ampelopsis* offer a treat for wildlife.

Even in autumn there are usually late roses still well worth seeing in the gardens and numerous vines, especially in the Italian Garden, although admittedly some of the grapes they produce are not as tasty as others! The Dahlia Border also maintains its interest throughout autumn and is complemented by the magnificent display of statuary which forms a sense of continuity in an ever-changing scene.

As you stroll through the gardens you may be lucky to catch the mouth-watering smell of the Katsura tree (*Cercidiphyllum japonicum*), which has a wonderful toffee-like or candyfloss aroma complementing the beauty of the heart-shaped leaves that are orange and pink in autumn.

The 'Great Storm' of October 1987, which swept through large parts of southern England, felled more than 1,000 trees in the gardens at Hever. Most of these, if not all, have now been replanted.

Left: Outer moat. Above: Pompeiian Wall, Italian Garden.
Facing page: View of the lake from the Loggia.
Overleaf: Loggia and Piazza with island in background.

Left: Aerial view of Castle with Italian Garden, island and lake in foreground. Above: Detail of child's sarcophagus (Roman).

WINTER

As winter approaches, the warm red bark of the redwood trees glow against the winter sky and the malus and quince-like medlar fruits glisten in the frost. The last of the red and purple leaves of the magnificent Crimson glory vine (*Vitis coignetiae*) fall to the floor, creating a multi-hued carpet underfoot.

The majestic hellebores nod gracefully in the winter sun and the witch hazels and viburnum begin to bloom, a sure sign that winter is drawing to a close and that spring is on the horizon.

The yew topiary stands majestically on the way up to the castle and becomes especially striking when it is tinged with frost or dusted with snow. If you are lucky enough to see it in moonlight, the silhouettes create an almost eery presence in the gardens.

The gardens at Hever are home to an ever-changing display of wonderful plants and structures and the collection is constantly being enhanced. One fascinating recent addition is the Wollemi pine (*Wollemia nobilis*), one of the oldest known tree species in the world, dating back to the time of the dinosaurs.

Much of the statuary and sculpture in the gardens is more than 2,000 years old and was collected by the Astor family in 20th century, along with the diverse collection of trees which includes tulip trees, handkerchief trees and Indian bean trees.

Far left: Loggia. Left: Topiary Walk. Facing page: The Nymphs' Fountain made by W.S. Frith in 1908 and inspired by the Trevi fountain in Rome.

Top: Tiger Lily bedroom.

ASTOR WING

When William Waldorf Astor purchased the Castle in 1903, he decided it was not big enough to accommodate all his servants and guests. Extending the Castle posed a unique problem as it was surrounded on all four sides by a moat. He rose to this challenge by creating a wing on the other side of the moat in the style of a Tudor village and connecting it via a covered bridge.

The Astor Wing is still used today and is available for hire all year round on an 'exclusive use' basis for weddings, conferences, day meetings, company 'away days', product launches and private dining events. Like the Castle, Astor spared no expense and the largest of the areas in the Astor Wing, the Tudor Suite Dining Room, features beautiful oak panelling, making it a stunning and unique venue for private lunches or dinners. The Tudor Suite Sitting Room provides a more intimate atmosphere for up to 24 guests and makes a very romantic backdrop for civil wedding ceremonies. Both rooms, along with the Tudor Suite Breakfast Room, overlook the idyllic Tudor Suite lawns and outer moat. They are often used for corporate meetings and private drinks' receptions alike.

When the Castle itself is closed to the public, the Inner Hall and Dining Hall can also be hired as an historic and memorable location for wedding ceremonies, receptions, corporate and private events.

It is possible to stay in the Astor Wing just like many of Astor's rich and famous guests would have done when he hosted weekend parties. There are 21 individually designed bedrooms which can be booked as part of a function. These are offered only on an 'exclusive use' basis, so the accommodation is both peaceful and quiet. Facilities available to guests staying in the Astor Wing include an outdoor heated swimming pool, tennis court, croquet lawn and billiard room.

Information about holding an event in the Astor Wing can be sent on request.
Tel: 01732 861 800. Email: tudor@hevercastle.co.uk. Website: www.hevercastle.co.uk

Far left: Tudor Suite Dining Room.
Left: Music Room.

OTHER ATTRACTIONS

Shopping The Hever shops offer a unique shopping experience for everyone, with a beautiful array of exclusive gifts, souvenirs, local produce, children's toys and a large selection of books. Estate-grown plants and shrubs can be purchased at the Potting Shed.

Eating Visitors will enjoy the warm and friendly welcome in the award-winning licensed Pavilion and Moat restaurants, which serve delicious freshly cooked hot dishes, afternoon teas, sandwiches, snacks and drinks throughout the day. The restaurants are also available to hire for private celebrations.

Miniature Model Houses A unique collection of $^1/_{12}$ scale model houses, which was commissioned by the current owners of Hever Castle, from the master English miniaturist furniture maker, John J. Hodgson. The models are set in a permanent display and journey through medieval times to the Victorian age.

Adventure Playground Shaded by mature trees, children up to the age of 14 years can let off steam in the enclosed wooden playground. There is a variety of wooden climbing frames, swings, slides and the Tower Maze. Equipment for the under fives is also available.

The Yew Maze Measuring 80 feet by 80 feet (24.3 m by 24.3 m), the hedges reach eight feet in height with almost a quarter of a mile (0.4 km) of pathways inside. It is one of only a few traditionally designed mazes in the country.

The Water Maze Situated on Sixteen Acre Island, the maze consists of a series of concentric stepping-stone walkways sitting over water; at intervals the hidden water jets spring into action to soak the unwary visitor. Few reach the grotto in the centre without getting wet; however, it is very popular and challenges young and old alike.

Lake & Rowing Visitors can discover the local wildlife including kingfishers, swans, herons and crested grebes on the hour long nature walk around the 38-acre (15.4 ha) lake. At the foot of the lake lie the waterfall, weir and three WWII pill boxes. Traditionally built rowing boats can be hired from the boathouse.

Events Hever Castle plays host to a variety of special events throughout the year, including the annual jousting tournaments with the Knights of Royal England, medieval weekends, gardening events and half-term activities.

Hever Castle Golf Course Hever is an idyllic setting for a championship 18-hole course, a 9-hole course, driving range, practice facility, large professional shop, bar, restaurant, sun terrace, function venue and civil marriages. It is considered to be one of the best golf courses in the area.